Saffron Dreams

Pardis Aliakbarkhani

ISBN
978-1-990416-01-9 (Paperback)

To my namesake across the sea and across the city.
To my beloved friend Javed Mohammed
and every member of my found family.
I love you all.

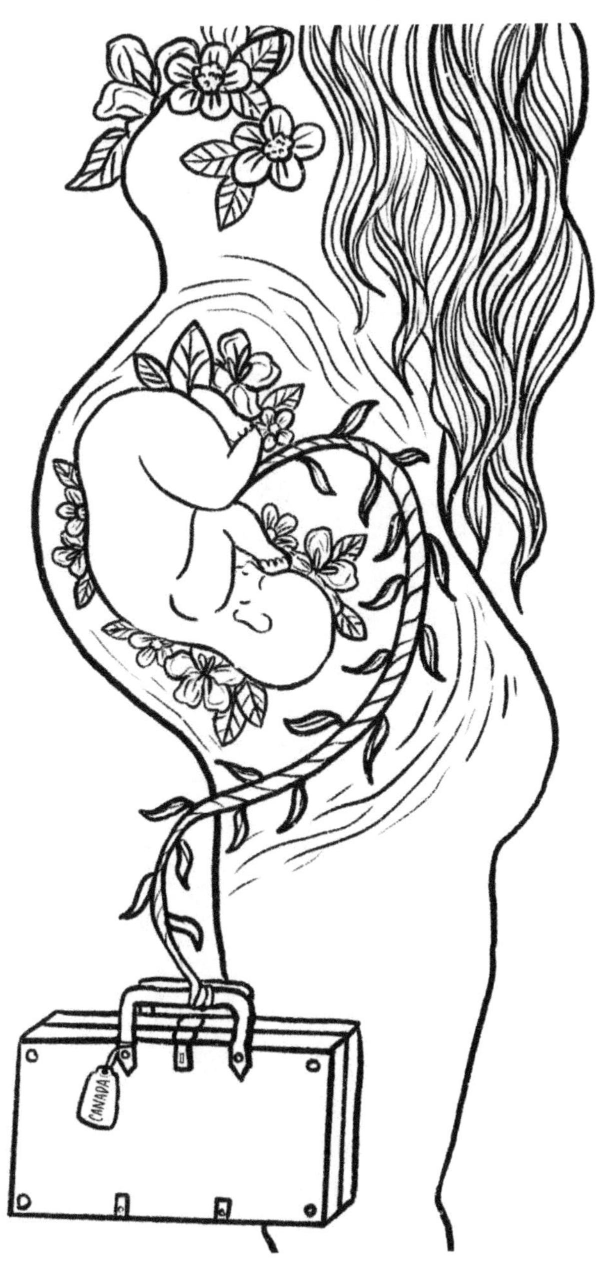
CANADA

Contents

Dearest reader,
Welcome to this meeting place
Between pages of white
The words here are my own
May they offer you hope and light
When you travel through this book
Know that darker roads
Are promised too
The Middle East is an enchanting place
With some nights deeper
Than the darkest hues

Part One

Sweet Saffron Dreams

So many people can inhabit one body
Shift in vertebrae
Exorcised only by passing time
When one triumphs and dominates
See, I lived in a house of bone and flesh
Spoke blood into the air before my veins
I nurtured different guises to survive
To mature from childhood unmaimed
Soft and meek for a heavy hand
A bark and bite for peers with sneer
I became who I needed moment to moment
Shifted frames until in wholeness
I disappeared
Yet little by little
When safety wasn't a fabled place
I started to change, I reclaimed my thoughts
From fractured becomings
I formed my own face
A chameleon to survive then
A second skin still to live
I've been born twice in this life
Once in September
Once liberated from dichotomous strife

When our elders ascend from this life
Become a vapour
From what was once blood and bone
History leaves with them
Knowledge that lives in the spirit
Is designed to be passed down
Loved into our kin
So that we do not lose ourselves
From losing our ancestors

Fire the coals, ready the wood
A feast is alight, meats on a skew
Tomatoes blister their skins and burn black
Sit atop a bed of rice
My mother offers onion and herb
Not once, twice, but thrice
Tarof is a love language
That stretches your belly with each meal
As grandmothers and aunties fill your plate
With lipstick kissed into a blush on your cheeks
Food is love
Food is community
Food is nourishment
Food is medicine
Food is history
Food is liberation
This food, this moment
Is everything

Persians know how to say goodbye
In three parts; a yawn, a look
And a final chat by the door
Fiddling with keys and shoes
While pouring chai again
For a story they forgot
Promises to see each other
Half planning when and where
Many kisses more in between
That despite tiredness, in friendship says
Lingering in doorways,
"I wish this night would never end."

A woven rug sits under my feet
As I weave myself into resting comfortably
I cross my legs, knot them into lotus pose
A desert flower sprung up from wool
Our host sprinkles cardamom in our tea
With black leaves suspended
In a hickory-coloured sea
Rose water too, tickles my nose
As the tea I sip pours down my throat
My comfort grows
My belly warm, my chest too
Somehow from a loving tea
I feel renewed
I glance at my father, my sister, and kin
How simple this moment would look
Without knowing the depth of feeling
Stirring, pitting, evoking from within
These moments are a blessing
A fragment of history that remains
A joy that we still carry
In distant, foreign plains

Prayer sung in song
A heavenly hymn
Reciting dreams to our gods
Answering a call from within

Every colour paints this land
So many faces unite Iran
Black Iranians bordering the sea in Bandar Abbas
Balloch Iranians from northern mountains across
Kurdish Iranians with red hair
And fire in their eyes
Turkic Iranians that share the same beaming smiles
The land that connects us
Has divided us too
Forgetting the spirit of our diverse groups
The history that has raised cities
Out of shared tongue
Bore dialects that still survive in fringes
No one is lesser than the next
Iran is but a mosaic
Made richer for its differences

Run your hands over my skin
Like the spine of fruit
That you can't wait to break open
And sink your fingers into
Taste me on your tongue
Let me linger there too
Until you can think of nothing else but
The sweetness you can't undo

Laughter is our dearest medicine
My people laugh through our pain
Through war, famine, lashing-games
It is our humour that keeps us sane
How my sides split when I am close to tears
Imagining my crumpled face
And impeding frown
I think of what we've survived in these years
Massacres that emptied towns
A silver lining finds us still
As the darkest of clouds brew
My people joke and laugh through the pain
Washed in waves of tears and laughter
To be made anew

Our hips speak a history
That cannot be silenced

So much is lost in translation
How could I begin to say
What sparks commonplace
On one's tongue in Iranian
Makes little sense here, a world away
In this departure
I find myself forgetting, too
The joy of our stories
That live in those roots
How do I explain that my sister
Calls me her dearest
By calling me her liver?
Apart from maybe
Saying that I am so dear to her
In spirit
That I feel almost as essential
As the body

Rose water mists, a passing trend
Gohlab for 2$ on the market stand
Bottled and branded
For the masses to consume
For the modest price
Of 18.22$

A lunchbox of dread
As I pulled it from my bag
Eyes shut with a prayer
For something subtle and bland
A crustless sandwich with ham and cheese
Or white bread with jelly
Oozing from every crease
But instead I had a container
Of piping hot ghormeh sabzi
My favourite when I'm at home
Not at school where upturned noses
Had spare eyes to look
Eyes that narrowed with question
Noses that wrinkled with disgust
A savory stew of herbs
Kidney beans, dried lime
Beef cooked soft
Over much time
This is what I had over a bed of rice
The taunting may have been easier
If I'd paraded around with a head full of lice
Even then, I couldn't help but smile
At the note that was tucked inside
"I love you, daughter. I love my two girls.
You are my sunshine.
You are my whole world."
The words were spelled wrong
With a smiley face scrawled
But it reminded me that my mother
Packed this food with love

Lamb blood paints the floors
When a new heir is born
Tradition that honours sons and daughters
Before their eyes open to the world
The meat is cooked in celebration
Feeds a small village in its sacrifice
A death to welcome the living
Split between bread and rice

I cut my lip
On the edge of his jaw
Let him witness me like a barren tree
Before the night and its stars
When he studied me with eager hands
Tracing over the map of my skin
He discovered countries in me
That I hadn't yet stepped in
Love is the finest adornment
To make it is the most human thing
That a woman's worth should diminish
While a man's remains unchanged
Is fractured morality

I found my voice
When I realized I could not break cycles
Before breaking my silence

Close your eyes
Imagine feeling the sun on your face
Rays of warmth kissing your skin
Into summer hue
Sweat beading at your temples
Rolling down the sides of your face
The sound of the sea in your ears
Waves crashing over rocks
The salt in the air floating into your nose
On the roof of your mouth, your tongue
Children laughing
A breeze cooling you momentarily
With a breath of relief
Your eyes open to families with their gaze
Looking towards the same horizon
Mesmerized by the same waters
Of the Caspian Sea
Where sturgeons lay gold
In turquoise depths that seem deeper
Every year, despite the water receding
Imagine the secrets this water once held
The ones it still does
Memory that survived oil spills
War, drought
That healed itself time again
That exists to remind the people
Who touch it
That we can be born again
Many times in the same life

We do not simply say
"I miss you"
Iranians say
"Delam barat tang shodeh"
Which translates, loosely
To "My heart tightens for you"
That the void of your presence
In my life
Can literally pull my heart strings tighter
Can summon an ache unparalleled
Is more than I can say for love
Than an expertly curated ballad
That your essence
Has left me in such rapture
That even in your absence
Your carry my heart in your hand
With your fingers clasped around it
Brings me to my knees

Suckle the Saffron nabat
Offer the dates
Welcome the pouring tea
With glasses held high
Fill fruit into your plates
My home is the home of peace
When you enter this door
You become family
Even strangers are friends under my roof
As I pour them chai

My father wrestled stubborn goats
In the mountains
Before leading them back to the barn's hay
Herding them towards feasts of grain
And water in an oblong tray
They'd nudge him awake
When his eyes grew dreary
Like a pied piper summoning goats
They trailed after him daily
The babies they'd bear
Already recognized his face
From the sound of his voice
They'd conditioned his name
Into the image of man
They bellowed and galloped
Over my grandfather's land
Our farm of the dusted mountains
My first home in Iran

Character is currency
My word is my bond
When all else evaporates
The spirit cannot dissolve

Barbari noon
Feta cheese, tomatoes, cucumbers
Nuts and seeds
Parsley, mint
Rows of herb greens
Curated breakfasts served with
A pot of scalding tea
Saffron sugar crystals
Melt into our mugs with glee
Simple breakfasts with family
Sat around each other
Meeting in shared glances
In tender care
In good food
Reconnects us to each other
So that in two ways
We become full

Hairy arms
Hairy thighs
Hairy brows
That furrow when you cry
Hair paints my body
In nature, not sin
I've learned to shed my body's shame
Instead of the hair that grows from it

When you are born
And when you are delivered
Are two separate becomings

Cards spread before my mother
On the settee
I ask a question that raises my heartbeat
I keep the words locked under my tongue
And my mother shuffles the cards again
Before tapping them
She lays them out
Begins her run of solitaire
As the succession runs
The answer becomes clear

Kiss my cheeks
Not once, but twice
If you love me enough
Find them for a third time
A greeting so simple
Yet the warmth it radiates
Could keep me in summer
Through bitter February

Sometimes the English language
Catches in my mother's throat
And she fumbles the words in her mouth
Until she spits out Farsi in their place
Tongue-tied
Searching for home

Sometimes I find a 'softer' name
To substitute
The one I was given at birth
That on English tongue sounds harsh and brute
It gives me comfort
An idle disguise
So I can navigate conversations
Bypassing "ifs" "whats" and "whys"
Something simple, common to local ear
Helps to quell my own budding fear
I adopt this persona
To catch my feet on equal ground
Even when I know myself
A name is not a curse
I should tip-toe around

Freshly pressed dollar bills
My mother irons before the New Year
Crisp as she hands them to me
In an envelope she has signed and sealed
Elders pass money and gifts on to us
At the spring equinox
When our world turns yet again
Flowers returning from the winter frost
Wealth is green in twice over
When flowers bud to bloom
Bouquets of 20, 20$ bills

I place a lot of importance on
The kind of ancestor I will be
Future branches on my family tree
Are watching me now through memories
What I do now
Who I choose to become
With speak in legend
As leaves form for the next generations

My first dose of sexuality
Came from an illuminated scene
Back when static clung to your fingers
When you touched a computer screen
A French drama I streamed online
That culminated in a kiss between housewives
When their husbands were away
Fighting for a politician's lie
I remember that confused yearning
How I gasped at my desk chair
Checking over my shoulder desperately
To ensure no one else was there
Such things are so forbidden
For a culture obsessed with touch
Two women and two men could
So often embrace that it would arouse
No suspicion
But this passionate display
Was more than our brand
Of unbridled friendship
Or two men holding hands
This was heat, this was longing
Hell, this was damnation without apology
Yet for the court of public opinion
That condemns more than it grants mercy
It confirmed a suspicion deep inside
I had been scared before to claim
That I lingered on a woman's lips too long
I gazed at her collarbones with a sigh
I wrote love notes to boys in class
As my heart stopped pressing up against

Another girl's thigh
For all the scorn I knew I'd face
A comfort settled over me still
An explanation for this curious fascination
A weirdness I hadn't given a name to
Now I know that despite
A cloaked man's perception
Or public scrutiny
That I am no less sacred
Or less Iranian
For being who I've been born to be

I imagine the first Canadian winter
My parents experienced
After their long journey from home
How did the cold wind bristle their bones?
My father landed in Canada
On Christmas Eve
To the chagrin of border agents
Who just wanted to clock out and leave
"You had to come today? Really?"
One scoffed and then sighed
My father, weary and frostbitten
Simply replied
"We didn't know."
Maybe a "sorry" slipped in, too
He must've been overwhelmed
After the travels he'd endured
What did the snow feel like, I wonder
On the brown of his skin?
Did snowflakes twirl over his brow
Dotting there like sweat crystallized
From nothing?
Did an uneasiness turn his stomach
Leave him standing, naked, empty
Like a winter-stripped tree?
Did he look out onto the white plains
And think of my sister and me?
Did he see through the flurries
And imagine his new life?
Did he see he'd become a father?
Did he imagine meeting his wife?
Maybe the potential he saw

Was a blank canvas, a clean slate
His first Canadian winter
Becoming the backdrop to rewrite his fate

Dig deep into your soul
There are countries in you to restore

On the southern coast of Iran
Boats come to port in bands
Reflected from the water, wares from far reaches
Pile into merchant carts, to be sold at markets
By the beaches
Women in red flowing dresses and battoulahs
Walk along the sand
Their piercing eyes cutting through
The hungry gaze of men
The salt of the windy sea air
Unfurls curls from their coverings
A twisted curl waves with their fabric
Blending into the sky and the summer heat
So much beauty in the land that carries us
The water that connects us to the world
The south opens our country's arms
To wonders once unknown

To be soft in the right hands
Safe in my vulnerability
Could make me feel stronger than anything
That is the problem
With the way we reserve our tenderness
For funerals and calls too late
We are a culture that acts
As if it is always preparing for war
And in that way
We create battlefields out of our homes
Thinking that our hardness will protect us
Even when it becomes the force behind
The shrapnel embedded in our skin

The farvahar rattles on my chain
Swings on my chest
Tangles in my mane
A symbol of our old gods
A spirit, conjured winged thing
Transformed from religion, in time
Into a cultural remembering

The sun spit fire
Into my throat
So I could break chains
With the flames my ancestors burned in

Hands holding hands
In a circle we dance
A fire burns into the night
Flames speak seduction with red tongues
That lead us into trance
Alight are the faces of my brothers
My sisters
Elders weave into line too
Strength in our unity
Our feet shuffle in tune
We move to the beat of a drum
The plucking of a tar
We travel circles-far in rhythm
In the path of our ancestors

My mother says "I love you"
In prayers, in cut up fruit
In the way she dreams my dreams
Even when she doesn't understand them

A woman's place
Is anywhere God can see her

The holiest book I ever read
Were my sister's arms outstretched
Pages spread that said,
"I will embrace you in every form."

We wash the rice
Until the water runs clear
Starch rises to the surface as fog
But soon disappears
Rice welcomed me home as a child
Nourishes me still as an adult
Soaking up stews and curries
It exists without fault
We wash the rice
Until the water runs clear
Jeweled with pomegranates, carrots, and almonds
As versatile as it is dear
Rice canvassed against so many cultures
Some distant, some near
The complexities may differ
Yet in all, the water runs clear

Let your daughters take up space
With their bodies, with their voices
Let them be athletes with imposing figures
Staunch politicians
Unwaveringly curious scientists
Let them be the future
Without apology

Mermaids live in the water
Of the Caspian Sea
They are Anaihita's daughters
Purple-haired sirens with fish feet
They whisper songs over the the waves
Where families walk the shoreline's sand
Scarcely showing their faces
To their cousins on land
They protect us with their prayers
The magic of their fins
That with a kick, soften tides
Leading sailors to the port of friends
And of those lost to the salt of sea
The mermaids watch over them
The dead reborn as mer family

Persepolis
Remnants of our kings of old
Prophecies written in stone
Worth their weight in gold
Celebrating the new year
We pile food into baskets
For a picnic by the old center's grounds
In celebration of future tidings
Hoping for blessings
To make our ancestors proud

Bury me in moonlight
Rest my eyes with the stars
So that I can dream with the heavens
And know those I love who have departed
Are never really far

A bustling bazaar alight with colours vibrant
Filled with vendors' goods teeming in piles high
The street beaten down, paved with foot traffic
Families walking in rows
Mothers holding small hands
That reach for fresh fruit
Spices caressing senses: sight and smell
Silks and fabrics strewn over lockbox tills
Breadmakers' yeast rising
Bread born in stone ovens
Waft over from a nearby windowsill
Rugs hung up like a living will
Our people wove these threads
With generations of wisdom in each band
A tapestry of our land in ornamental design
Oil lamps and mosaics
Glass glimmering in the light
Treasures from the West of Turkey
Smuggled in during the night
Men play shatranj
And break seeds between their teeth
Sipping tea and laughing as rosewater
Perfumes the street

Coals burn on punctured aluminum bed
Smoke rises from a coal disk's head
Our water pipes sit in rows of coloured glass
Water bubbling with every puff
We pass
Tea and dates sweeten our dry mouths
Before we purse our lips to blacken
Our lungs again
A circle of friends wreathed
In circles of smoke
Legs folded over woven rugs
Secrets sitting in the air between chosen few
We find comfort here and clarity
Through a fog of coal

Fruit stands bursting with colour
Ripe enough to taste in the passing air
The billowing fabric of a farmer's cart
Perfumed by their sow with flair
You pluck a handful of cherry plums
From an overflowing bowl
Pop them into your mouth
Where their sweet and sour flavours swirl
Two worlds combine in your palate
Not unlike the contradictions of this land
A city of culture so vibrant
Patrolled mercilessly into reprimand

Kindness is King
Holier than all
More regal than any crown
That has graced any brow

The rhythm of our hips
Will sing chorus at wedding processions
With hands raised in the air high to the heavens
Our people move with the beat
As bloodlines remember
The celebration of pouring into streets
When a union is entered
An Auntie raises a handkerchief
Twirling it as her pitch rises
Bubbling from her lips: a zaghrouta
Laughter as the night becomes us
We are joy and joy bodies our kinetic melody
In these moments of pure splendor
Dancing is our second tongue
A gift, in time, fond memory

Saffron fields
In mid-October they brighten their bloom
With stems that strain their necks
To form rows of purple hue
In their congregate, waves in the wind signal
A pedestal sown from vine
To applaud the summer blossom
You must first praise its green spine

I wish I inherited more cunning
Than kindness
So I could navigate this world
With less bruises
Then I think that my kindness is a birthright
That my open arms mimic the motions of love
That brought me to life
Through generations of compassion
That cradles me still in the acts of service
The community my family has built
Despite their suffering
We are bruised and beautiful architects of survival
Displaced from one garden
Building and taking root in new ones
Connected in the end
Not by the soil or the battering that shook our leaves
Loose from their stem
We are connected by love
Love that is the root of who we are

You can die so many times
In the same lifetime
Without ever having really lived
That's why my parents taught me
To dream when I am awake
And bring every fantasy I can
To fruition
Because sometimes nothing in this existence
Is promised
Except for suffering

I part my hair in two
Flatten curls with a heavy brush
I weave two plaits of braids
Massaging oil into each strand
As they slide between my fingers
I hum a familiar tune
One that my grandmother sang
When she braided her own hair
She wore her braids as a school girl
Until she near nestled herself into the grave
Her hair carried a tune of sacred divinity
That her fingers followed on instinct
And years of conditioning
When I look at myself in the mirror
I see her smiling back at me
With a song's memory splayed on her lips

Glass pendants of blue hang above our doors
An evil-eye, all-seeing, protects our souls
I wear one around my neck
Some in the beads of my bracelet
Imprinted in my mind, my consciousness
Are circles of blue, a sea of eyes
That reflect the world's evils back to their kind

Henna on my hands
In a dream that I have
The night before my wedding
In a city in Iran
The smell is familiar
Half flower, half earth
The paste mixed into a bowl
Dried consistency like dirt
This soil comes to life
When water meets its powder
It transforms into decorations that
Kiss my skin in colour
An artist takes my hands in hers
Draws flowers, a small bird
In delicate manner she takes me, a canvas
To become her work of art

Bread: a food, a utensil
The smell of sunrise
The labour of nimble hands
Baked into comfort itself

Recipes are written on my mother's wrist
She seasons our meals with her heart, not eyes
Or measurements
When she steadies her hand
It's like the ancestors have stepped in
Held her to stop and said,
"That's enough there, dear one."

The Simmorgh is
But the part of our souls
That yearns for growth
And is willing to pay growth's toll

My childhood was curated by Persian rugs
And giving my father massages
By stepping over his back
Kneading his sore muscles with my timid feet
Like playing hopscotch over skin
For the driveway we didn't have
My parents gave me everything
Or as much as they could
As much as they knew how to give
Rather than lament on what I didn't experience
I choose to remember the magic of what I did

Anxious airport visits
Watching arrival signs light up
Family waiting at gates
With hand-scrawled love notes
While the other half of them climb out of planes
With suitcases filled with gifts from home
Silver, silks, saffron, nuts, and figs
Meeting finally to read posters held high
That say "Welcome."
But mean
"I love you. You are my home coming home."

Lavashak sour on my tongue
Fruit leather as addictive as an illicit drug
How I pleaded to my mother at the market
For a little, just a taste
How I peeled it from the wrapper
With fumbling fingers in my haste
Pleasures from my childhood
When things felt simpler
When the world, in my eyes
Could be healed with a taste of fruit leather:
A bit of sunshine

The altar on our new year
Summons love and prosperity
Coins welcome money
Greens that we call sabzeh
Usher rebirth and host longevity
The intricate display of 7 items
Are but wishes for the sun's next turn
An apple for beauty
Garlic for the health, the healing
For which we all yearn
The altar on our new year
Is more than tradition
But living history
What we hope, we erect in 7 tokens
The essence of haft-seen

Prayer didn't make me feel closer to God
In the darkness when my self disappeared
But meditation had me meeting myself
On alternate edges of the cosmos
Brought me closer to salvation than any holy book I'd held

Talks with family back home
After burning through a stack of calling cards
Booming voices and lines breaking up
Passing the phone to aunts, uncles, and friends
Grandparents meet us for the first time
In our voices and broken Farsi
The yearning to stay connected
Split by land and sea

Figs, figs, figs
Sweet with the nabat in my tea
Figs figs figs
Warmth that lulls me to sleep
Figs, figs, figs
In dreams that never leave me bitter
Figs, figs, figs
The voice of my father, his deep timber
Figs, figs, figs
He holds me like a baby
Figs, figs, figs
I cradle his memory

When all the world is softened by sleep
Wrapped up in dreams and sheets
I look out to the moon and think of you
Where across the sea
Your sun is rising
I wonder if you feel the sun's warmth
And think of me, too
Letting her rays kiss you when I cannot
Enveloping you in the kind of embrace
That lingers, enchanting your brown skin
Creeping a blush to your cheeks
As natural as what I feel for you
Without warrant for crime
The only punishment is how I miss you
In the long nights so far away
No noose tempting my neck
For the 'sinister' disposition
Of being gay

My heart beats with lambskin
Stretched into a drum
A chorus of pounding
An ancient rhythm
When I forget my purpose
Or my place on this earth
I put my hand over my heart
And feel the beat of my birth
I was born with divine purpose
To give back to the culture that raised me
I can feel the past and present
Through a single heartbeat

Money spills onto the counter
When we go out to eat
Credit cards slam down before a waitress
After a family morning tea
We argue over who gets to pay
With such fervour
That other tables' patrons crane their necks
To overhear our clamour
In our families we often can't agree on much
Except that we all must have rights to pay
For this morning's brunch

Daughter of Anahita
I feel reborn in the water
Every mineral in my body
Restored by salt borders
With every wave I am washed
Even in the shower I hear her whisper
That all is not lost
My people will be delivered
But even deliverance has its cost

My parents worked themselves
To the bone
To bring us in from the cold
Hid their tiredness in smiles
That I mimic now as an adult
My parents starved their dreams
So that my sister and I
Wouldn't have to go without
The only way I know to honour
That sacrifice
Is to live my truth loudly
And without doubt

Part Two

Less-Sweet Dreams and Nightmares

Have you ever had soldiers
Beating down your door
In plain clothes
Like a neighbor you can't ignore?
Barreling into your home
Crushing the essence of comfort
With their heavy tread
As you console a child with promises
You can only hope are true
Like, "It's okay, they won't hurt us."
Cooing soothing tones, in a whisper
In a prayer
To wash over the erratic beating of your heart
To drown the fear in your chest
Before it surfaces in the eyes of your family
As guns threaten their field of view
The real weapon being the fear
That lives in you
Years after you crossed the sea to freedom

Saffron dreams curate pictures in my mind
The sweetness of a pomegranate seed
Juxtaposing the bitter of its rind
Music playing on a lambskin drum
People dancing at the foot of fires
Illuminating them
Festival and merriment
A drunkenness that almost tastes like freedom
Families huddled together
Their laughter a second song
The stories of our elders
Lined within our own palms
An imprint I don't recognize, then
Officers crashing through thresholds
Without welcome or cause
Policing morality with batons and bared teeth
When they are more animals than gods
With the brutality of their belief
Divorced from God
The simmering chai, made sweet with golab
A rose thorn on my tongue
Grows from the grief of what's lost
Farsi is the first language of my people
Courage the second
Though fear patrols the streets
Intent on breaking them
The days are longer than before
With little Sun in sight
But the Saffron dreams of my eyes
Liberates my people into the light

Imperialism knocks on our door
With a smile
Before burning our cities down

They want our oil
They'll massacre our land
Our blood feeds the soil
Where their boot soles stamp

When a plane struck the side of a building
It brought the world to its knees
And dusted an entire city with its ashes
Buried people in it
Even the ones who survived
Died in part that day
Never to be resurrected the same as before
A world over
A war came to the doorsteps of merchants
Of healers
Of farmers
Of housewives
Who had never seen a plane in the sky
War crashed into their history
With a force tenfold
Than what penned September
In the lived memory of millions
And how could they begin to grieve
For the losses they suffered
For crimes they did not commit
When the world closed its eyes
To their pain?
With armies dispatched
Not for justice or freedom
But political gain

Imagine the fear
Of compacting your entire life
Into a suitcase that you shuffle
Into the night
With smugglers whose names change
When the sun rises again
Men who know borders
And the shadows that penetrate them
Lead you through the wilderness
On faith alone
Faith in a stranger that took
Your crumpled up bills
And your parent's tears as payment
To help you reach the other side
Of a border wall that was never built
With guards patrolling the countryside
With guns, eager to shoot
For little more than the taste of blood
Imagine running in the dark
Your heart beating in your chest
As if for the last time
Imagine holding your breath
Convinced it would be the last time
Imagine standing on foreign land
For the first time
Knowing that you could never go home
That is just the beginning
Of what my mother endured
So that I could be free

Borders are acts of violence
No one should be turned away at port
Beaten away from refuge
We all belong to this earth
My home is your home
No one is illegal
Under God's roof

Mental health in the Middle East
Is a silence that hangs between
Family branches
That at its climax
Strikes like lightning and breaks wood
Severs branches
Without care for what would've come to bloom
If only we could have shed our shame
And replaced it with understanding
Reminders that illness is not a sin

When a loss is dear enough
A family's blood can water
Their own loved one's graves
Grief has cut through more bloodlines
Than swords have

Sometimes I feel the stab of shame
When I think about the homeland
Where I inherited my name
For a culture so vibrant
A history so rich
We can be so cutting
To those we see as different
The judgement that curls our lips into sneers
From smiles that once spread ear-to-ear
To our kin of different colours
A hierarchy we create
To our neighbors on either border
That some regard with hate
So prejudice is our conditioning
That in modern age, it simply makes one sick
To imagine we've come so far in knowledge
Yet regressed in perceived politic

Masked men can spew their vitriol
As readily as the acid they throw at a face
But the women of my country
Are strong beyond their grace
And these cowardly men
That hide in the fear they try to arouse
Know that a woman with an education
Trumps a gun with endless rounds
Every open book, every page that turns
Unlocks another barrier, then another still
For a young girl
So it's not that they believe women
To be the lesser, a second class
Rather, they've realized the power we possess
And that makes them scared
As perhaps it should
That a woman is not an object
But claims her own personhood
Women are fiercely intelligent
We are kind
We are brave
And the only way these masked men
Think they can diminish us
Is to stunt us through our pain
Yet we cannot be broken
Or silenced through the currency
Of their fear
We deserve equality
And we will accept nothing less

If violence has any place
In how you choose to practice your faith
You are relying on the devil's tongue
And not God's wisdom
To guide you

My mother left her home
To escape religious scorn
Beatings that would reduce her to ash
Burnt like a sigil of unwelcome form
As if God has favourites
As if threat of pain sustains glory's name
That one should risk imprisonment, torture
Or death
Should they worship in a different way
To live is to love
To be kind is the holiest declaration
But that way of thinking
Has not yet impregnated the thought
Of the leaders of my nation
Instead lash scars decorate our elders' backs
The ones that could survive
The graves of others are desecrated
Their tombstones broken and scattered
Into piles
Is this your decree?
Is this your holy protest?
That neighbors can set aflame their countrymen
At a black cloaks' behest
Your words are poison
Your actions deadlier still
If you should find your way to the afterlife
Your deeds will only open the gates
To hell

I convinced myself that
The distance between us was in language
Not love
But when you speak callousness
I can hear your heart beat in echoes of hate
And I need no further translation

I love my family, my culture, my home
They are like limb to me: my blood and my bone
Yet toxicity is not alien to us
We are not so removed from critique
Because we exist in minority
I struggle with this—the need to protect
The homeland, my people
Yet, in there, is regret
Why am I so compelled to protect
A country
That does not acknowledge me?
A country rife with corruption, sexism, racism
And religious supremacy
I want to raise my voice and my fists
But not to become a symbol
Of Western disgust
I don't want my words to inspire
The racism that already has its eye fixated
On the East
How can I reconcile these two demands
To demand my people be better
Without inviting Other hatefulness?

When you paint your wife
Black and blue
Do you see the devil
Reflected back at you?
When her body trembles
At the sight of your hands
Does it quell the need inside you
To feel like a man?
So commonplace
Is a battered wife
That back home many wouldn't blink an eye
Until it is their own daughters
Their sisters
Nieces
Or friends in kind
Whose skin becomes a masterpiece
Of a man's perceived slights

Reyhaneh
I hope that heaven opens its gates to you
With applause
That in eternal sleep
You meet the peace you could not make
Against a tribunal of manly law
I hope that the clouds you step on above
Are lighter than the paths you had to tread
While the world watched and pleaded
For the staying of your death
I hope the sun shines on your face
Drying the tears you have cried
I hope that God embraces you
As she should have in life
I hope you feel safe, finally
Knowing your body is yours in claim
Knowing that to women like me
To resist sounds like saying your name
They wanted to make an example out of you
Out of women who decide to fight back
So that they can levy their own assault
Pervert their own attack
They dreamt your death would inspire silence
Force women into smiles for slithering hands
But we are more bold for your rebellion
We refuse to cower for the comfort of men
Sleep, dear sister
Take your peace
You will not be forgotten
By women like me

Middle Eastern women
Are labeled exotic and curated in gaze
For the consumption of men in the West
Who would sooner bomb our borders
Than learn our traditions
We being as foreign to them
As civility

I wonder
When our parents beat us into submission
Do they see their own fear
Reflected in our eyes
Do they remember cowering before
The hands that promised to protect them?

The walls of my childhood home
Were paper thin
But thick enough to conceal our suffering

A child is not a vessel to carry family secrets

Screaming matches bleed out our front door
How we're taught to love with war
Family rituals of gritted teeth
Passing years feel like defeat
What to do with all this rage
This bitterness only distills with age
Waking up to the sound of raised voices
I crawl back into bed
My sheets like forged trenches
I've never understood how the violence
Could escape me
Until I remember to dream without sleep

Revolutions can gestate for years
Before being born, restless
For the world to see
For the world to hear
Raised fists and raised voices
Demanding freedom
Calling for justice
Too long denied
In the stumbling first steps
Of cruel leaders
Inept at leading their people
From years of looking down on them
Instead of walking alongside them

Middle Eastern history did not begin
With western imperialism
And end
In 9/11

We poke fun at our parent's accents
In English
They do the same for our mother tongue
Both languages influenced by our rearing
In different nations
But if I heard a stranger laugh at my mother
Or ridicule my father's pronunciation
I think I would split their humour
From their spines
And send them back to the Creator

I grew up with my mother
Cinching my body with her eyes
Inspecting everything I ate
To shrink me down to a respectable size
Advice from her friends
Felt less friendly and more pointed
When my body became an open forum
For their collective disappointment
Queries fell into my ear
Before I even entered a room
If somehow a pound shed from my body
Everyone already knew
The congratulations, the welcome I received then
Was unlike anything I'd felt before
As if losing 20lbs was comparable
To a soldier returning home from war
On the other hand, when I gained weight
My first year of university
Family gatherings felt to become
A chorus of weight loss retreats
My body carried me through all these years
Through heartbreaks left unspoken
It survived me through
The chaos of my upbringing
Helped ensure my spirit remained unbroken
Yet despite all this, my body deserved no praise
Because it didn't fit the mould designed
By a certain gaze
And the judgement it received
For simply being carried
Rivaled a hatred I hadn't known

So, in the end
The duty to love my body
Has been all my own

I don't owe anyone my conscience
Or my time
Even if their blood flows through my veins
Like honey wine
'Love' has been instrumental
To so much abuse in my life
That I forget what it sounds like
When it's played in sincerity

Men back home like to label women weak
Until it is women in troves
Liberating cities
When pictures of the Yazidi women
Filtered through my phone screen
It was a photo-proof of a waiting truth
That many had yet to see
Famed for our obedience
Yet, in war zones we stand
Freeing cities from terror, in our rebellion
Cleansing Mother Earth and her land

Mother
Auntie
Woman with eyes grazing me
With judgement
Nose wrinkling with disgust
A conditioned prejudice
A tongue sharpened from years of hate
Justice to you
Would've been you studying your body
With kindness
So that you could understand your womanhood
As a friend and not an adversary
Something to be ashamed of
Your sexuality coiling within itself
Until a pair of fumbling hands groped for it
On your wedding night
You should've been free to experience your body
As a vessel for love, for pleasure, for joy
Not a prize forfeited after a lifetime of chaste
You taught us what you knew
What women of your time
Were taught to understand
That a woman is only as valuable as she is pure
And that any action that provokes
Her own pleasure
That derives from her own autonomy
Is a stain on her character
That she cannot wash away

You grew up cradling your dreams
Against the backdrop of warzones
I believe that's why you
Sometimes raised us as soldiers
Instead of children

Prisons do not disappear injustice in Iran
As much as they pay tribute to it

I think about what it will be like when I meet my own daughter someday. Will her hands curl into fists and raise into rebellion? Will she be a quiet spectacle that nurses revolutions in the silence? How did you envision meeting us? Did you fixate on our dressings – who would inherit your upturned nose, your soft hands, your glimmering smile? Instead, did you wonder who would have your quick wit, your contagious laugh, your attunement with every growing thing? I think about what it will be like to meet my own daughter someday a lot. I don't care what she looks like. I don't care if she is completely strange to me and everything I've ever known. I can only hope that I am strong enough to embrace her, truly, for who and what she is. I hope I understand that she is an ever-evolving concept, the details of which are beyond my control. I will remind my daughter that I am merely a guide. Open arms. There to hold her in any shape she could take.

'Be realistic' is a phrase that would never touch
My brother's ears
When his ambitions enter a room
No one would question how his career
Would rival his ability to love
Or sully his title as a reverent husband
A doting father
Fail to feed the seeds of family into fruition
Adding another heavy branch onto our family tree
Aunties would not look for signs of his youth
Souring
Study the lines above his brow
Like an expiration date
Wrinkle their noses at him
As if he is curdled milk
His dreams could be so similar to my own
Only he would not be punished for having them

Sex is not sin
Sex is divine
It is a means of worship
When two bodies collide

The world I had read about as a child
Is dissolving from memory
Leaders grapple for power at tenuous times
Latching onto fear to quiet the noise
Of a knowing rebellion
Fear is designed to feed the machine of war
Words are the first guns in battle
They make enemies out of strangers
So that it becomes easier to shoot
Easier to shoot a monster than man
Disappear cities in a hail of bullets
Fire round after round
Breaking the barrier of sound
With impossibly fast execution
Before a pair of bootstraps has time to ask,
"What am I fighting for?"
Deafening conscience with campaign drivel
Words like 'unity' that mean 'division'
I realize now that the world
I had read about has never existed
History has always been penned in blood
By self-righteous victors
Who shape the narrative to suit their means
When they were the disease
That spread across nations
Dropping bombs
In the name of Gods they don't answer to

Heaven's door is buried in the sand
Where bodies are a crumpled heap
Where the sky has swallowed cries and delivered bombs
Instead of salvation

What consolation could you give a country
So touched by war
That clinging to the side of an ascending plane
Feels like the last chance to cling to freedom?

There is nothing a wicked man fears more
Than a woman who is not governed by fear

Resistance is restorative
Boundaries are sigils of closeness
Warships are punitive decree
Poured into metal molds
Rubble from broken cities nurture fertile soil
Destruction is birth
From which we live again and again
Even in death

The economy of peace does not serve the West
When riches live within the borders of the East
People disappeared by the violence of war
Are casualties for men
Who lead with the knowledge
Of the value of everything
Except that of human life
Fighting against leaders opposite the world's end
Who speak in different tongues
But answer to the same language?
Hungry for the same power, fueled by
The suffering of their own people
Their heartbeats resurrected
By dollar signs, forgetting
Gold bleed from the Earth can't be bartered
At Heaven's gates

When fear threatens my resolve
Softens my once rigid spine from protest
I feel my sister's hands lace along my back
Then my mother's
Then my grandmother's
Then women who share my passion
But not my blood
Sisters in spirit that have known the acid
Of swallowing your own tongue
They hold me higher, taller
And I project my voice with the courage
That reaches them
Across the sea and above in Heaven
Where warrior women retire
From a lifetime of visible and invisible battles

The Middle East is a land marred by war
Fruit trees watered by bloodshed
Their yield tumbling
From weakened family branches
With the devastation of bombs that collapse cities
A place of beauty and pain
Where tragedy sits commonplace on ears
Like a song we've heard too many times before
Tracing over maps that become like scar tissue
Before we can remember the comfort of "home"

Family secrets have carved up my tongue
Into a dagger intent on cutting cycles
Umbilical, born and breed
That have fed me before I knew life
When I speak, I untether myself
To years of pain I refuse to inherit

The walls in our home
Have been painted with lacquer and tears
Witnessed so much rage unraveling
From years of neglect
That sometimes I feel them sink
From trying to hold us up and together still

Evin prison
Is so peopled with intellectuals
That one of its broken wings
Is referred to as 'Evin University'
That alone has taught me everything
I need to know
About how justice flies, elusive
In the borders of our skies

I am exhausting myself
Trying to reconcile the reality
Of being my father's ambitious daughter
And recognizing that I am not defeated
For deserving rest

Easier to try to fit in
Than to explain
Why I feel so out of place
Not Canadian enough
To tap maple from my veins
Not Iranian enough
To not choke over common phrase
Caught in the middle
Of a cultural divide
On one hand I love my birthplace
On the other I grapple with
Ancestral pride
A longing for two places
Two worlds
That I exist between
Remains the greatest caveat
Of immigration rarely seen

Attendance calls in the morning
A teacher with a dubious look
Narrowing her eyes to read the letters
On the page attached to her clip book
Without hesitation, I raise my hand
"It's me," I say
Flushing into a cherry red
A weak smile touches her lips
As she nods in acknowledgement
Peels of laughter from the class follow
As I sink into my chair with embarrassment
A name I grow to hate
Though it was my first inheritance
A resentment I feel for my parents
A resentment for my heritage
In the years that follow my hand precedes
The teacher's attendance attempts
Before they sometimes even have a chance
To butcher my name
Cut into it with colonial tongue
"It's me," I say
Until one day I speak up
I pronounce my name for them
I say, "I am Pardis Aliakbarkhani"
And all the snickers recede
Because I have no shame left to feed

Our mothers and aunties
Pour the tea
Before spilling the tea
Never cautious for where it will stain

Your parents can be pillars
But not gatekeepers
For your self-worth

Leaders whose minds are imprisoned
By ignorance
Imprison their people
By iron
Eldest children
Becoming second parents
To siblings
When they themselves have not
Had a childhood
Is adolescent injustice
A heartbreaking but all too common crime

Persia died in 1935
When the name Iran was born
To please 'Aryan' tribe
A scar on our history
That is hard to ignore
To be complicit
In the face of such atrocities
To allow leaders that deny them still
To represent our land and country
That is a bitter pill
That to be better
We must swallow whole

Some argue that the man in red
Is merely covered in soot
That he plays songs for the New Year
After tending ancient fires, in a red suit
But the ring of his chains
Caught heavy on his ankle bones
Rings of something different
A crime for which we have yet atoned
Who would want to believe it?
Face painted black, lips maroon
He sings to children in a familiar tune
Red, red, blue
Red, red, blue
Shackled he stays
To keep the lay people amused

Acknowledgements

This book has been a journey and a homecoming. It has allowed me to connect with parts of myself and my culture that I have longed to reach for years. In reading this, you have come a long way with me. I hope we meet again. Like this, between pages. Somewhere soft, safe, and sacred.

Thank you to the ancestors that guided me through this process and continue to guide me in all my endeavours. I feel your strength in my spine and your enduring warmth in my heart. I hope I grow to be someone worthy of your namesake.

Finally, thank you to Hana Shafi (a.k.a Frizz Kid) for the beautiful cover art and illustrations in this book. Hana is a Toronto-based creative whose work explores themes such as feminism, body politics, racism, and pop culture. More about her and her work can be found at www.frizzkidart.com

If this book spoke to you, I would love to hear from you. Feel free to write a review, connect with me directly on pardisaliakbarkhani.ca, or on social media @pardisalia

www.ingramcontent.com/pod-product-compliance
Lightning Source LLC
Chambersburg PA
CBHW051807050726
47598CB00006B/2458